# Draconis

Nereia Crisan

BookLeaf
Publishing

Presentation by *BookLeaf Publishing*

Web: www.bookleafpub.com

E-mail: info@bookleafpub.com


ISBN: 9789357213752

First edition 2022

*to all the angels in my life*

*(you know who you are)*

# ACKNOWLEDGEMENT

No project of such dimensions can be finished without giving thanks to the people who made its finalization possible – all of them are wonderful individuals who have all my appreciation and love.

To begin with, I would like to thank my parents, for being there, very close (too close) every time I was writing or agonizing over writing. They stayed with me through failed publishing attempts, through college applications, through exams, through frustrations caused by the lack of creative juices; they were pillars, quite often. Parenting is not easy and I know they think it's beautiful, but I could never do what they do – so, for that strength, I am forever grateful.

I would also like to thank my publishing team, of course, for providing the opportunity for me to finally allow these poems to see the light of day and for the public to enjoy it for themselves. #TheWriteAngle challenge that Book Leaf Publishing provided was a launching ramp for me, creating the path for this book to reach you.

Lastly, I would like to thank my friends, who, for 5 gorgeous and messy years, have always been there, annoyingly close or annoyingly far, in warm presence or on a blurry screen. They stole my personality, I stole theirs and I wouldn't change a thing. In all of your weird, flawless glory, you are one of the best things that ever happened to me. Love y'all; especially the Trio. Stay crazy forever!

Big thank-yous and hugs to all

# PREFACE

Poetry is quite often overlooked as an art. It can be seen as lesser, because of its length and falsely perceived lack of complexity, or more complicates than prose due to the intensity of the feelings conveyed. I'd beg to differ against each of those claims by arguing the other. A poem may be short, but the magnitude of this art lies in the skill it takes to encompass a multitude of feelings that we sometimes don't even have names for in just a few lines.

I was introduced to poetry by accident, during middle school, in a relatively mundane English class. We read a poem by Carol Ann Duffy, "Valentine", which opened my young, eager eyes to a very different literary concept that wat I was used with: beauty in the ugliness of the world. Duffy compared love to an onion, a multi-layered monster that imprints on the person that wields it. I was haunted by this idea that the most beautiful things in life can be found in tragedy, in heartbreak, even in death. There is a very simple reason behind this – this type of beauty is not unnatural, is not sublime, not on a superior, perfect plane of existence. It's painfully human and painfully relatable – which is what poetry should be.

Most people dislike poetry because they deem poets as obnoxiously morally superior. I think that those who harbour such perceptions miss the whole point of this craft – which is to provide accessible feelings wrapped in pretty words to people who struggle with their own sentiments and the maelstrom of confusion that comes along with them. As a young girl approaching womanhood, change can feel daunting and desirable at the same time, which is an appeal love and the idea of afterlife hold too. Two years ago, at the beginning of a very long summer, I had an idea for a poem – which was something completely new to me. I had written some (albeit, not very good) short stories before, but poetry was still a murky, deep, scary lake for me. The idea was not fantastic and my first poem even less so. My following poems were me playing with concepts and prompts, just to find what fit me best. It took almost a whole year for me to find that what drove me were stories – different characters and lives, dancing around in my headspace, making blurry films and loud music. I knew I needed to get these raw stories on paper, and prose could not achieve the level of abstract beauty I required to tell them properly.

This collection is an apotheose of my artistic work so far, having selected the most heart-breaking, visceral imagery that I came to appreciate in art. I chose to give the name of the serpent to this anthology, as testament to the birth of knowledge that poetry can bring to mankind. We don't give the legendary snake enough credit for giving us what we needed instead of what we wanted – I am honouring now that deep, hereditary need for knowing more, for exploring, for wandering.

Welcome,
Nereia

December 2022

# draconis

your green ribbon
wrapped around the old apple tree's roots
your clear laughter
echoing in the morning dew
your bare feet
waltzing over the slippery stones by the creek
your sun kissed head
bent to listen to a whispered birdsong

you hold my hand
grass entwined between our laced fingers
you feed me buttered bread and ice-cold wine
you kiss me with your sweet strawberry liqueur
mouth
and the sun still doesn't set
the sun never sets

I notice the scorching heat too late

your green ribbon
is the snake pouring venom in the roots of my
brain
your raucous laughter
turns into a reverberating cackle
(the garden is a cave

and the water in the creek looks dead)
your bare feet
wantonly dance on bloody, clanking skulls
your grinning head
bent to listen and check if my heart still beats

after a heartbeat or two
you pull it out of my chest
and feed it to the hungry ravens up in the hollow
apple tree

# pomegranates and salt

I think it's funny
how I don't believe in redemption
but if I had to choose between
all the sinners and the saints of this world
the monster I'd save is you

like a faithful dog, I lap up any kindness you
offer
and mistake your bemused smiles for love

I drank the darkness seeping through your lips
your teeth bright, wicked stars
I ate the last crumb of it, I sipped the night
just so I could feed you light
(it burns you, though
it burns too bright)
I wonder if a cowering demon
is worse or better
than an angel of serene wrath

my mortal flesh cannot contain
the impurity of my love -
my spirit sings in exhilaration and tragedy
each time it brushes yours

the words we say are dancing close to heresy
the words we mean are blasphemy
(the things we never tell each other are
borderline lethal)

# liminal spaces

I'm stuck in a limbo of perfection and yet always
wanting more
I am a star outside of any constellation -
I let my god down
and took a new one for a lover
(our love story is my new benediction)

the taste of ichor is too similar to liquor
for me to claim I can't find meaning
at the bottom of a bottle -
it's all dust in my mouth
so unlike the ghost of your bright smile still
tingling my lips

your presence is a suicide pill
poisoning me gradually
you explode in figments of memories and
what-ifs
I implode in my own rotten soul
and the ruin of my black heart collapses in on
itself

oh, the thrill to be finite
and yet feel so much
(too much)

oh, the tragedy to be infinite
and yet never have enough
(never enough)
what shall I do with all this leftover love?

# tell me about where the white dragons live

tell me about the clouds over the mountains
where they dwell
tell me about the silver wolves guarding their
cave
tell me all of it
until I get sick of the sound of your voice

we spun fairytales till the hours turned long as
days
and the moon shone brighter with each unspoken
word

what would night be with no murderers to aid?
what would dawn be with no bodies to uncover?
what would night be with no sweet illicit affairs?
what would dawn be with no lovers to break
apart?

we practice necromancy every night
but we couldn't revive this love -
not without missing bones or crooked limbs

you fall in love with everyone you see
much like Apollo before you

but don't you know you burn like the last sun at
the end of the universe
leaving moth ashes and broken hearts trailing
after you?

# plastic lighter to your unlit cigarette

I have a flame eating at my heart
I'm a fire tearing at the very fabric of the world
you're pure gasoline
the ebb and flow of my veins
black as coal, beautiful as death
always shifting -
we were made to unmake each other
to build a chaos so high there'd be no one left
but us

every touch of your icy fingers on my flushed
skin
was a torch dropped on my kerosene heart

I think I understand it now
what you were trying to tell me last summer -
I'd have whispered it back in your ear every day
for the rest our lives
if I could have swallowed the bile in my throat
then
and said it before night fell

you unscrewed something inside of me that day
I couldn't look at you

your bruised lips and bruised heart were too
pretty
I was caught in the headlights of this unspoken
thing
it was like wild sun rays on my undomesticated
retinas

I didn't miss the irony
of your favourite song playing on the radio
as the car drove away from you and the sunset of
the summer of my life
(although I wish I did)

# I didn't kill any of them

I buried her myself
(I wasn't at the funeral)

I couldn't watch her lifeless corpse
(I wonder if I'm the one who killed her)

he kisses me softly on the mouth
and I think he doesn't know the garden is a
cemetery
(I wonder if he'd still kiss me
if he knew my lips are full of the dirt beneath her
cross
and the tears of her lifeless eyes)

she breathes in my earth, he breaths in my ear
she strokes empty branches with ghost-like
fingers of wind,
he strokes my ego and my naked ribs
she lives in me, he might soon not live at all

the earth is alive, unlike her
and soon it will swallow us whole

she died on a wednesday, we got married on a
thursday

and the church bells drowned out my heartbeats
but not my guilt

soon, there'll be another funeral
her soul feeling sorry for me from heaven
her body laughing cruelly beneath the soil -
and the silk rimmed coffin will take him too

I buried him myself
(I wasn't at the funeral)

I didn't kill any of them
(rightfully so, no one believes me)

# something like a prayer

for you, I'd eat an apple
my only innocence swallowed down
ripe sweetness from my mouth flowing onto
yours like nectar -
bruised lips, red and trembling, still fluttering
with love
(you'd smile at me brightly
hold my hands, touching anything but the
fingers that held the fruit
and say "darling, you shouldn't have")

for you, I'd cut my wings off
my only redemption ripped in half
placed on a silver platter as a sacrifice for your
shrine -
black feathers, bloody and broken, all fluttering
with love
(you'd kiss me on the forehead
stroke my back, touching anything but my scars
and say "darling, you shouldn't have")

for you, I'd set a church on fire
my only salvation burning at my feet
exorcising myself while you dance away your
purity -

charred skin, tattooed with ash, still vibrating
with love
(you'd fly me away from the ruins
bathe me in holy water, touching anything but
my heart
and say "darling, you really shouldn't have")

# I'm sorry I chose him

the snow is only half melted
dirt and white blend on the pavement
the money you gave me for the cab back home
lie in the grime of the city that killed our love

(who are we kidding?)
it wasn't the too bright lights shining in car
windows
it wasn't the night sky birthing grey mornings
it wasn't the glass of tall buildings
it wasn't even the text I never sent you
(it was the string of texts I never showed you
that weren't addressed to you
when they should have been)

winter is no colder than my heart
(the cab taking me home should have crashed)
I spoke to him and talked to you,
spent my evenings in a darkened room
and ran from your light
like a too easily burnt moth
(you are a butterfly with clipped wings -
I pinned you down to keep you on the
empty canvas of my heart
and flying away tore you apart)

I was the one who left
and yet the frost doesn't bite
harder than the consequences of my actions -
I miss you so bad
and I barely even left...

the snow hasn't covered my tracks yet

# metempsychosis

you're beautiful
like a broken spyglass
like a crumpled love note
like a shattered window
or a crushed rose

they'll hang you by your wings
a grotesque windmill in the eye of the storm -
I wash away the ashes of past lives from your
burnt fingers
I baptize my favourite pilgrim

I'll sing you lullabies that I have never heard
I'll sing you through this rite
that neither witch, nor priest knows

you're beautiful
like Adonis in the night,
in the way only a tragedy
played on a moonlit stage is

from the belly of the beast
emerges a seraphim
hurling their juvenile wings at odd angles
hoping to fly from birth -

I keep washing away at tendons, spines and
collarbones
a caricature of the painting with
the virgin and the messiah

# hiraeth

summer is ending
and the last embers of the august sun are dying.
summer is ending
and I broke your heart -
september can only bring rainstorms and your
tears

the wildflowers in your bouquets
the wildflowers you put in my windswept hair
the wildflowers by the edge of the road
where we'd meet every day -
I'm wilder than a thorn bush
and you should have known I'd draw blood

the red of your cheeks
when I first kissed your skin is vibrant
against the image of your now pale face and
angry eyes -
(you told me you loved me
and I didn't say it back)
don't you know all beautiful things born in
summer
die in autumn?

# panem et circenses

I welcome you to my table:
bring nothing but your hunger and your appetite
let me kiss each of your apple-white teeth
and cherish them like pearls,
let me kiss your apple-red lips
and drink up your laughter, manic and sweet,
soluble venom on my parched tongue

you kiss my throat like the bones beneath are
honey-sweet
a whole swarm of bees in my mind
buzzing like pagan thoughts

falling in love is an instinct as ancient as raging
at gods
as old as an infant crying out for milk
as old as the string tying the stars together

we're curved towards each other like a pair of
faded apostrophes
the beginning and the end of something too
magnificent for a name
we're two immaculate white ribs taken apart
from the same primordial torso
and begging to be fused back together again

give me back my heart, you defanged serpent
keep my heart forever, you wingless bird
a nightingale feasting on raw flesh and flashes of
love
a snake whose blood ran cold for far too long

# hectic waves to steady moon

I wouldn't trade the best years of my life
for the fantasy of unrequited lips -
I would hold onto my memories
if I couldn't hold onto you
I'll have the version of you you'll give
instead of a sweetly fabricated knock-off
or a supernova-shaped hole in my door
from when you left and never looked back on
me,
forever stuck lingering in the back of my mind

a darkened sky, no stars
maybe we weren't star-crossed
just drawn together, hectic wave to steady moon
destined to never collide
but change each other
as if change were the most natural thing in the
world

you always go too fast, always running
a perfect perpetuum mobile,
an engine too sleek for its car -
yet you are the only constant
immovable lighthouse
in this bay of doubt, danger and secrets

loose lips sink ships,
yet I talked too much and said too little
our boat may be floating but the water laps up to
our chests
black waves drown out heartbeats
maybe I should've shouted it to the heavens
maybe I should've taken it with me in hell
maybe, maybe, maybe...

# Babel

two actors in love about to pick their masks
and pretend to hate each other for longer than
they could bear -
we hid from the truth like bats from sunlight
and forgot how to fly solo in the dark

I hear my manic voice
but you just hear me growl and howl -
Babel must have fallen again
and all the symptoms found shelter on my burnt
tongue
no animal was banished from the garden but the
serpent
all food tastes like dust
so maybe I was the skull under your hill all
along

I'm choking on the roses you bought me
the velvet petals hurt more than the thorns
I was used to pain like a dog to a leash
I don't know how to handle satin kisses or open
eyes
so I hide beneath smudged eyelids and
childhood trauma
uncertain if I want you to understand

# apostasy

the only thing sadder than
a broken heart
is a dying god
who has no afterlife to go to
no second chance
no sweet remembrance
no shrine
(we can still worship a dead love,
but without the smallest relic to cling on to
how can we still pray
to a spirit that is
more human than us?)

golden statues of animals we don't know
stone arches with warnings in letters unseen
putrid holy water
why is memory fickler than a heart?
(can I love something I've never known?
I can care for something I've forgotten)

temples without meaning
days with no name
traditions with no history or roots -
I'd rather lose faith than love

# early spring blues

last week,
I asked you if you'd go with me to a funeral
(you've been with me to every wedding,
you've seen me at my best,
I suppose it's only fair to see me at my worst)
you say yes, of course
(I could marry you, you know -
we'd get married in a church with no windows
saying our vows until the day they bury us)

we drive to my hometown
in a borrowed car
looking at the dark dawn and wishing
it was a bright blue afternoon

they carved their names into the wall
and in time, the blue wallpaper draped over them
rotted away
(lovers, parents, grandparents, dead)
two people lost in time,
two names lost forever -
we're the only ones who know,
the only ones who understand
that the blue wallpaper hides both past and
future,

that their names are only shared by us
(we could steal their marriage certificate
and call it ours)

forget-me-nots blossom on their grave
(I swear I won't forget,
you don't have to make flowers bloom in winter
-
I have the only miracle I want and
you're right here by my side)
forget-me-nots blossom in snow,
the same forget-me-nots my grandma planted all
those years ago

when we get back home,
after my first day at work,
I'll find you painting the living room light blue
and the crease on my forehead that screams
confusion and amusement
will not show how much I'd weep
for your understanding -
you know I love blue, I always did

and when I'll see the forget-me-nots by the
window,
I'll cry for real in your warm arms
and it will feel like home

# cosmogony

why did a swan have to fall for a comet?
a fragile wing, ready to break from the weight of
its own bones,
ready to let go and fall in a blazing crash
alongside its love –
there's something to be said about swans and
mating for life
but I think you already know

why did a bird have to fall for magnificence?
why did I have to be the one to die for love?
a meteor is strong - you could have borne it
better
every gentle word from you is a blow to my
twitchy flightless heart

I see swans dead in cages of icy lakes
and the Cygnus constellation smiles sadly from
above
at Icarus deserted by the sun

binary stars
we were meant to spin endlessly around one
another

until the universe dies and we're the only ones
left
we were meant to be in a solar system of our
own
yet you always craved another source of light,
brighter than my feeble moonshine

binary stars
two celestial objects that gravitate too close to
each other -
everyone can anticipate the magnitude of the
unavoidable impact

I can't wait to burst into flames with you

# apex predators

the fox stares down the barrel of the gun
the hunter stares down the barrel of the bottle
the rabbit runs to the moon
the crow flies to the sun
dark wings in too much light -
I wonder if this unnatural beauty is all you can
give me

I used to feast in banquet halls on bones with no
marrow
you drink the hunger away from my soul
and fed me honeyed steaks at your table

is it my mouth that fits your canines perfectly?
is it your hand that wipes bloody tears off my
face?
is it my face I see pale in the mirror
or do you just take up too much of my sacred
space?

do I want to be left alone?
do I want to flee?
you gave me the hills to run on
you gave me the rain to bathe in -
if I truly wanted to be alone

I'd have never let my demons fall for yours

31

# selling love in the big city

32

she rises like the blood moon
born a pathological liar whose half-truths are
meant to soothe

she tamed the monsters under her bed
before she even knew what nightmares are
devils sang to her in her crib
they taught her beautifully haunting melodies -
hell giving humans a blessing in the shape of a
siren

she measures her talents like a witch brewing
her love potions
shifting her charities to the highest bidder -
not the cold, impassive angelic chorus,
but the heartfelt singsong tale of a fallen host

she sometimes wishes she knew better what
tenderness is
but not too often
not all orphans dream of mothers -
some know better

# memento mori

I walk across an empty field thinking we could
have built our house there
a little cottage in which we'd bicker till we're old
and gray -
I aged a century in one year and there's still no
trace of "we"

I would need a lake-sized sink
to wash your blood off of me -
there's none left in me
I've been bled dry, my life gone
a vampire hurtling towards the light
depressed and defanged

I'm killing time as time kills me
I wander alone, waiting for the sky to cave in
me and my unfixable heart
there's not much left of it anyway
(there was no last kiss
and I have no grave to go to -
what did you expect?)

it's a bright spring out there
and I'm sunk knee deep in snow
wailing in an eternal winter

punching the ice until my knuckles paint the
endless silver red

born into this world with the sole purpose of
leaving it -
every single moment of every day we are dying
so what does it matter if another piece of me
died prematurely
because of you?

# oaths

we're in love with witnessing love
with basking in the beauty of the world -
each time we spit on it and flip it off
we fall for life even more

jumping up and down on a trampoline
I wanted to make you swear we'll be together for
ever
three pillars of salt laughing off the genocide of
the earth -
you said to not make pacts on a sunny day
and wait to see what the future holds

I was never one for waiting, but maybe you were
right

no oath was taken
no bond was broken
we'll still be here after a while

that's all love ever taught me
that's all I'll ever know -
calling this home is the only guilty pleasure I
can afford

I never grow tired of asking you the same
questions
and you giving me the same answers
I've always got bad things to say
you stick out your tongues, hold my hand
and though you don't tell me so, I know you'll
stay

when we die
promise me we'll haunt people together
promise me we'll sneak up on them, watch
movies on their tv and throw popcorn in their
hair
promise me the garden will never wither
promise me the record spinner will never break
promise me you'll be buried with your friendship
bracelet on, like me

# Philemon and Baucis

you coaxed me into trusting
turned an atheist into a firm believer.
you got me in for the long haul
for sleepless nights and restless days
to bear all life's sorrows with
a smile and a spouse.
we were children with big hopes
dreamers with big plans
and no matter how the gods rolled dice
I still caught your eyes and
you still caught my hand.
we'd meet in the garden
guarded by lanes of moonflower and jasmine
we'd meet on the pier
shielded by salty air and sapphire water
we'd meet in your mother's courtyard
that smelled of the apple pie she baked for my
birthday.
I bake pumpkin pies in november now
as we watch clouds pass and butterflies wither.
christmas waltzes and new year's kisses
on confetti and wine-stained floors, alone in the
dark
your eyes gleaming like olympic flames, my
breath catching

as if I ran for miles to
the finish line in your arms.
forever is humanity's most
beloved and treasured lie
but you still gave yours to me.
domestic dreams that weren't mine
wild journeys that weren't yours -
we did them all.
when we'll have no rooms to clean
no songs to sing
no countries to travel to
when we will be
too old to bear ill will, too young to remember
bury me beneath the linden you planted
shielded by your old denim jacket
from the sun of decades to come
I'll dream of you and our treehouse in the old
oak
I hope you'll dream of me, too

9 789357 213752